C000075468

GREATEST
Geordie
One-
Liners

GREATEST
Geordie
One-
Liners

Ian Black

BLACK & WHITE PUBLISHING

First published 2013
by Black & White Publishing Ltd
29 Ocean Drive, Edinburgh EH6 6JL

1 3 5 7 9 10 8 6 4 2   13 14 15 16

ISBN   978 1 84502 504 5

Typeset by RefineCatch Limited, Bungay
Printed and bound in Poland
www.hussarbooks.pl

A Geordie Two-Liner

Rumours that after the match the Newcastle United squad was seen successfully seducing young women in a Geordie nightclub with one-liners have been completely refuted by this month's manager, Alan Pardew.

He states: 'I find it totally preposterous to suggest that any of our players could make a successful pass to, or at, anyone.'

Geordie Questions

Yee hev the reet te remain silent, but yee don't hev the ability, dyah?

Yee sez 'no' te drugs,
did yee? They weren't
listening, were they?

Aye, sure, I'd leik te help yee oot, what way did yee come in?

Are yee into casual sex,
or should Ah dress up?

An which dwarf are yee?

10,000,000 sperm an
yee were the fastest?

Wi enough force, pigs fly
just fine. Want te join them?

Dyah still love nature, man,
despite what it did te yee?

Day ye want foak te accept
yee as yee are, or dyah
want them te leik yee?

I'm busy just noo. Can Ah ignore yee some other time?

What's yor problem, man? I'm betting it's hard te pronounce.

What am Ah? Flypaper
fa freaks, yee fat fool?

Nobdy likes yee,
surely yee remember?

Geordie
Pronunciation Guide

To the Southern ear, sounds like 'Ligature. Yeff gutter fierce lake appearer tets.'

English translation 'Look at you. You've got a face like a pair of tits.'

Geordie translation 'Lyeuk at yee. You've got a face leik a pair of tits.'

Geordie Threats
and Insults

The last thing Ah want te dee is hort yee. But it's still on the list.

Howay wee gadgie. Ye knaa
what? When it rains, you'll
be the last one te knaa.

Listen, bampot featchas, when yee were born they slung the bairn an kept the afterbirth.

Howay Yank, yee ur a
fugly futhermucker.

Ah thowt Ah saw yor nyame on a loaf the day, but when ah looked closer it sez: 'thick *cut*.'

Howay man, you've got a
face leik a cuddy in the huff.

That chin of yors looks leik
a dockah's kneecap.

When they were giving oot bellies yee jumped the queue cause yee thowt they sez jellies, didn't yee, fatso.

Yor feet are tha git big, tha if yee threw a shoe in the Tyne it waad be a hazard te shippin.

Wi those ears yee look leik
a taxi wi the doors open.

Cheer up man, ye've a face
leik a wet Whit Friday.

Yor bord's tha ugly, she'd
frighten a sailor off a raft.

If yee were a McDonald's
snack ye waad be a Fillet A'
Fish . . . Nobody likes yee,
but yee are always there.

WHAT THE HELL IS THA
ON YAR NECK? Aw, reet,
it's just yah heed.

Whatever keind of look ye
were gannin fa, ye missed.

Dinnit look at me tha way
or Ahl split yee in three
whole horfs.

Yor teeth are leik the Ten Commandments: aal nackaad.

Instant idiot. Just add alcohol.

Tesco needs yee.
They've run oot of stupid.

Ahd caal yee a fanny,
workie ticket, but yee seem
te lack warmth an depth.

Here's a pund, divvy, away
oot an buy yorsel a leif.

Pick a winda man, yor leavin.

If Ah agreed wi yee
we'd both be wrong.

Ah didn't say it was yor fault,
Ah sez Ah wez blamin yee.

Yee, plouk-puss, think
Johnny Cash is wha it
costs for condoms.

Yor teeth are leik a ra of bombed hooses – since 1944.

Away an iron yar face,
yee aad besom.

God must love sackless
foak. He made yee
an millions more.

I'd leik tae see things frem yor point of view, man, but Ah can't seem te get me heed tha far up me arse.

Ah divvent hev an attitude problem. Yee hev got a perception problem.

Yee, marra, are a waste of two billion yeahs of evolution.

If yee are looking fa
sympathy, radgie gadgie,
you'll find it in the dictionary
between 'shit' an 'syphilis'.

If Ah wanted te hear frem an
arsehole Ah waad hev farted.

Everybody has the reet
te be stupid, but yee are
abusing the privilege.

Yee are multi-talented, so
yee are. Yee can taak an
piss me off at the same time.

Yee hev got more issues
than the *Chronicle*.

Howay yee, aye, yee,
the oxygen thief.

Divvent annoy me. I'm running oot of places te put bodies.

When they put teeth
in yah gob, they spoiled
a canny arse.

Just cos you've got a
prick doesn't mean yee
hev te act leik one.

Divvent play sackless
wi me – I'm betta at it.

Yee are a spherical arsehole.
Ne matter which way yee
turn, yee are an arsehole
frem every angle.

I'd leik tae leave yee wi one
thowt, but I'm not sure yee
hev anywhere tae put it.

Marra, Ah could eat a boal
of alphabet soup an shite a
betta argument than tha.

Yee are just not yarsel
the dayuh. Ah noticed
the improvement.

Be yorsel? Bad advice
for yee, bonny lad.

Ah divvent knaa whit
makes yee tha sackless,
but it's working.

If what yee divvent knaa
can't hurt yee, then yee, lad,
are fucking invulnerable.

If yar brain wez chocolate
it wouldn't fill a Smartie.

Save yar breeth, nackaad
face, you'll need it te blaa up
yar girlfriend later on.

Yee hev got tha many
slates missing yee are
due a Cooncil grant.

You've got a gob on yee
leik a camel eating toast.

Yee waad be oot of yar depth
in a car pork puddle.

If ye were any more
sackless, we'd hev te
water yee twice a week.

If shite wez music, ya divvy,
yee waad be an orchestra.

Calm yarsel doon, bonny lad,
or Willie heor will show ye the
'knife in the daftie' trick.

Ahd bet money tha when yee
stayed at Michael Jackson's
as a bairn, he made yee
sleep in yar own bed.

Idiot heed? Yon makes
The Elephant Man look
leik Mr Univorse.

Shame aboot him. He's
marching te the beat of a
different kettle of fish.

Geordie Names

They caal him Compass –
his nose goes North an
his ears gan Sooth.

Baker ower there? The wifie an bairns are gone. Noo it's ernly him an his tart.

The Balloon is always saying:
'Don't let me down.'

He always makes a bolt
for the door when it's his
roond – that's why they
caal him Blacksmith.

The Depth Charge,
he's always affta a sub.

They caal him The Ghost –
always moaning.

Harpic? He's clean
roond the bend.

The Lame Kangaroo? He's not had a jump in yeahs.

Whenever Jigsaw is
asked te day summat
he gans te pieces.

Geordie Philosophy

Don't walk beheend me,
for Ah may not lead.
Don't walk ahead of me,
for Ah may not follow.
Don't walk beside me, eitha.
Just bugger off, waad yee?

Don't tyek leif so seriously, man. It isn't permanent – especially if it's yors.

Ah feel as if I've got a face
leik a dollop of mortal sins.

Just syah nah.
Then negotiate.

Whats for yee won't gan
bye yee, an yee desorve it,
yee divvy.

If yee divvent care weor ye
are, then you're not lost.

In Scotswood, it's sad hoo whole families are torn apart bi simple things, leik a pack of wild dogs.

I've got any amoont of
talent an vision an tha.
Ah just divvent gi a shit.

I'd crawl a million miles across nackaad glass te kiss the exhaust o the van tha took hor dorty keks te the laundry.

I've got the wisdom of youth,
an the energy of aad age.

One big voddy, two big voddy,
three big voddy, more.
Four big voddy, five big voddy,
six big voddy, floar.

Geordie Insults te Men

He's not sackless – it's keind of leik he's possessed bi a retarded ghost.

He's the keind of a fellow tha
ye could use as a blueprint
te build an eejit.

If he wez me dog, I'd
shave his arse an larn
him te walk backwards.

Them scars of his? A lifetime
of playin tiggy wi hatchets.

He's got a face leik a forty shilling piss pot – pure white, but aal chipped.

The ernly big thing aboot
him is his ears – he looks
leik an elephant wi the
wind beheend him.

Aye shame. His mam couldn't breast feed him – he wez cordling the milk.

Him, he's suffering
frem bottle fatigue.

Fat? He can sing a
duet on his aan.

Tha one! A lady o the neet once telt him sheh had a headache.

My Neville an sex?
This morning, Ah used
him te time an egg.

Him, he's got an IQ of two.
It takes three te grunt.

Ah keep thinking, if he talks enough, someday he'll syah summat intelligent. Am Ah holding me breeth? Ne.

Me gadgie is nay good
at sex, but he's thinking of
taking it up as a hobby.

Ah thowt aboot him aal dyah the day. Ah wez at the zoo.

Aa've had a really canny time,
but this wasn't it, yee gowk.

My Peter is good lookin,
the trouble is his teeth
are brighter than he is.

Ah will nivvor forget the
forst time Ah met him.
Christ knows Ah keep trying.

He's tha narrow minded tha
when he walks his earrings
knock together.

My Tommy? He's got hundreds of well-wishers. Everybody wants tae te hoy him doon one.

Sorry marra, Ah cannit put smaal objects in me gob or I'll chowk, man.

Him? The ernly playce he's ever invited te is ootseid.

A shag? Hoo aboot nivvor?
Hadaway an shite!

Ah will try bein nicer if yee
try bein betta looking,
yee gaumless gowk.

My Mick? Ye could use
his prick tae stitch tapestry
if it wasn't attached.

Geordie Insults
te Women

When sheh undresses
yee hear the Lycra breathe
a sigh of relief.

She's tha ugly sheh tried
te tyek a bath an the
water jumped oot.

She's cured hundreds
of Peeping Toms.

She's handled more
balls than Tim Krul.

She's been cocked
more times than Elmer
Fudd's shotgun.

She's seen more
stiffs than Quincy.

She's tha ugly, she'd
frighten a monkey oot
of a banana tree.

She's got a face tha could
myek an onion bubble.

She's got a face on hor tha
waad drive rats frem a barn.

She's got more chins than
a Chinese phone byeuk.

She's seen more Jap's eyes
than an Oriental optician.

It's leik shagging the sleeve
off a wizard's cloak.

She's tha bandy, sheh could
not stop a pig in an alley.

When sheh sucks a lemon,
the lemon pulls a face.

.

She's got an arse leik
a bag of washing.

Sheh wears enough
myek up te sink a ship.

Sheh sweats leik a dog
in a Chinese restaurant.

She's got a face leik
a stuntman's knee.

It's leik shagging
a pail of water.

She's seen more cock
ends than weekends.

She's tha ugly not even a
sniper waad tyek hor oot.

She's dun more lengths
than Duncan Goodhew.

Even the tide waad
not tyek hor oot.

She's got more fingerprints
on hor than Scotland Yard.

She's had more seamen
than the docks.

Wi a face leik hors,
every day is Halloween.

She's known as
The Olympic Torch –
sheh nivvor gans oot.

The canniest lass that
ever walked the streets.

She is a lass of rare
intelligence. It's rare
when she shows any.